Here is a Water Drop

Written by Elli Woollard
Illustrated by Irene Bofill Garcia

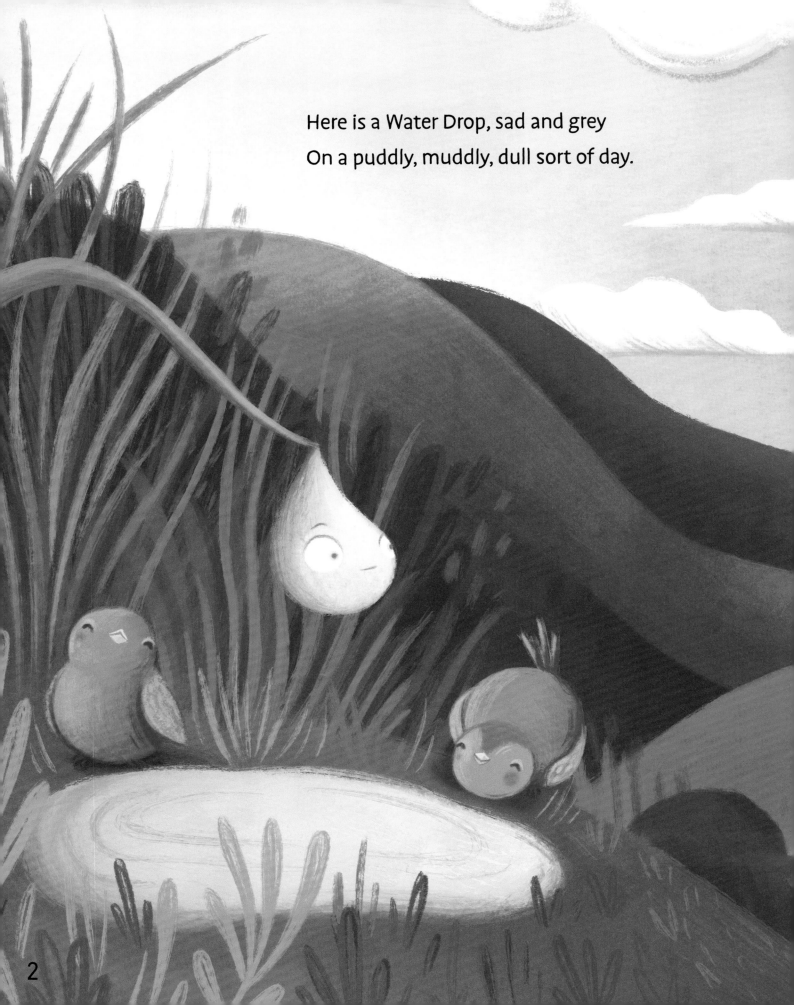

Here is a Water Drop, sad and grey
On a puddly, muddly, dull sort of day.

She sighs to herself, "How I long to be
In the shimmering, glimmering, silver sea."

3

Here is the Sun, bright and round,
Whose warmth lifts the Drop from
the pool on the ground.

Evaporation lets her take flight
As water vapour, small and light,
High over meadow and village and town.
But she thinks to herself, "It's a long way down!"

Here are the Winds, whispering, cool,
Which stop the Drop, and allow her to pool
With others like her in a clustering crowd –
Condensation has made a cloud.

The Drop no longer feels so small,
But she thinks, "Is there room in this cloud for us all?"

Here is the Storm with its biting chill,
Which tosses the cloud over mountain and hill.

But the cloud's too heavy – it's too much to bear.
Precipitation comes falling there.

So, soft in the light of the moon's pale glow,
The Drop dances down as
glittering snow.

Here is the Drop, frozen hard,
Resting a while in a small back yard.

And now she's a ball – she's whizzing – SPLAT!

Then she's a plump little man in a warm woollen hat.

But she dreams of the sea, sparkling blue.
Yet the sea's so far! And what can **she** do?

Here is the Sun, kindly, round,
That melts the Drop on the icy ground.

Infiltration allows her to seep
Through the soil, dark and deep.

She's groundwater now, slowly slipping
Off through the rocks, dropping, dripping.

She's buried for months. She wonders, then,
If she'll ever see light of day again.

11

But here is the Spring,
which leaps from the ground
With a babbling, burbling, gurgling sound,

And the Drop remembers
her sea-bound dream
As she rushes along on a
rippling stream ...

Through waterfalls crashing with thundering ROARS ...

And lakes that lap at their
shingly shores.

Then down the long miles of the river she goes,

And so, as it widens, on she flows

With such fearless strength, so eager, so fast ...

That she reaches the sea –
the sea, at last!

Now here is the Drop, feeling bold and brave

As she twirls in the swirls of an ocean wave.

"The water cycle," she thinks,
"is now done,
And my life of adventure
has truly begun!

The world is so wide! Now where should I go?"

But here comes the teasing Breeze ...

Oh no!

Published by Pearson Education Limited, 80 Strand, London, WC2R 0RL.

www.pearsonschools.co.uk

Text © Pearson Education Limited 2020

Written by Elli Woollard

Project managed and edited by Just Content Limited

Original illustrations © Pearson Education Limited 2020

Illustrated by Irene Bofill Garcia

Designed and typeset by Collaborate Agency Limited

First published 2020

23 22 21 20

10 9 8 7 6 5 4 3 2 1

British Library Cataloguing in Publication Data

A catalogue record for this book is available from the British Library

ISBN 978 0 435 20192 0

Printed in Slovakia by Neografia

Note from the publisher

Pearson has robust editorial processes, including answer and fact checks, to ensure the accuracy of the content in this publication, and every effort is made to ensure this publication is free of errors. We are, however, only human, and occasionally errors do occur. Pearson is not liable for any misunderstandings that arise as a result of errors in this publication, but it is our priority to ensure that the content is accurate. If you spot an error, please do contact us at resourcescorrections@pearson.com so we can make sure it is corrected.